Milkweed Matters

A Close Look at the Life Cycles within a Food Chain

Written by Lisa Connors
Illustrated by Betty Gatewood

Milkweed Matters

A Close Look at the Life Cycles within a Food Chain

Written by Lisa Connors

Illustrated by Betty Gatewood

To Chris for his patience and to Betty for taking the plunge with me. *LMC*

To my supportive family, friends and art instructors who have encouraged me
to follow my passion for art in the out of doors, to continue learning new techniques
and to pursue exhibiting my art. *BG*

The sun rose as it did every morning. Its light shone down on the brown soil and its energy warmed it. Underneath the soil lay a tiny milkweed seed.

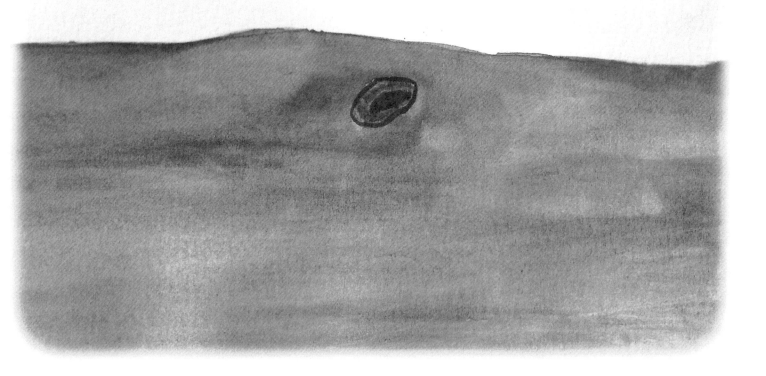

With the sun's warmth the seed began to grow. First, a root stretched downward.

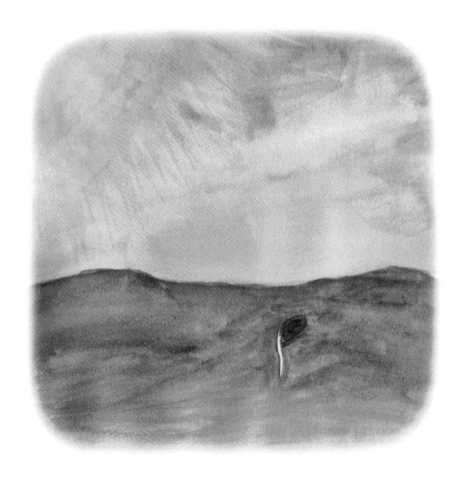

Then a leaf stretched upward until it broke through the soil. The milkweed plant kept growing because of energy from the sun.

That little seed grew into a tall milkweed plant. Its flowers were pollinated, maybe by a bee.

The flowers became seeds.

The seeds dropped into
the soil and the milkweed
life cycle continued.

But that's not all.

One summer day, a monarch butterfly laid an egg on a leaf of a milkweed plant.

The egg hatched and
a tiny larva, a monarch
caterpillar, emerged.

It ate and
grew
and ate
and
grew.

Where did that caterpillar get its energy to grow?

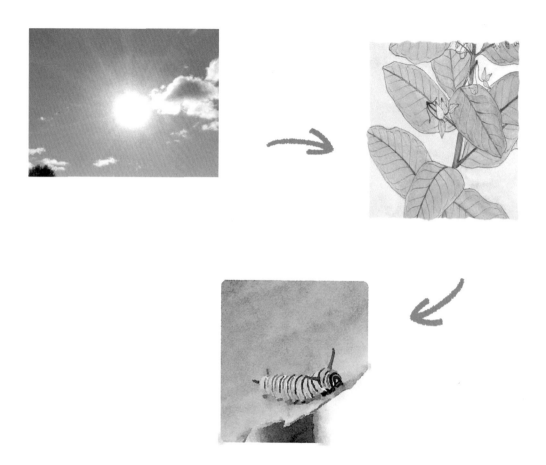

From the leaves of the milkweed plant.
The same plant that got its energy from the sun.

That monarch
caterpillar
grew and
molted and
grew and
molted, until it
was ready
to make a
chrysalis.

Inside the chrysalis, the caterpillar changed into an adult
butterfly. Its metamorphosis took about ten days.

The adult butterfly was finished growing, but it still needed energy to fly and find a mate. It got its energy from the nectar in the milkweed flower and other flowers. That's a monarch butterfly life cycle.

But that's not all.

Later in the summer, another monarch caterpillar emerged from an egg. It ate and grew and molted and metamorphosed into an adult butterfly, just like the other monarchs earlier in the summer.

But this butterfly migrated south to Mexico for the winter where it clustered with hundreds of other monarchs to stay warm.

One night a black-eared mouse in Mexico ate a monarch butterfly. The mouse needed energy to raise her litter of babies. She got her energy from the butterfly.

And where did the monarch butterfly get its energy?

From the milkweed plant, which got energy from the sun.

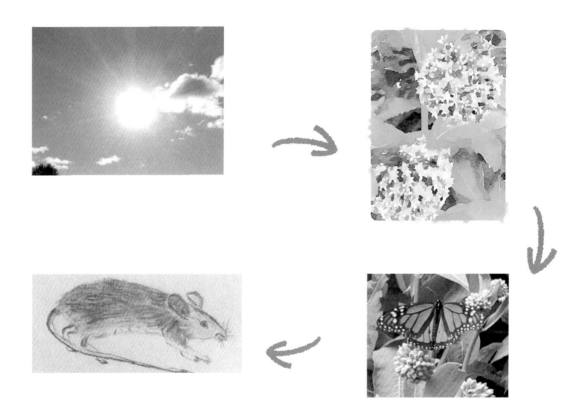

The baby mice ate and grew. When they were full-grown, they mated and had their own babies. That's a mouse life cycle.

But that's not all.

One day an owl ate one of those mice. The owl needed energy to hunt and survive. It got energy from the mouse. And where did the mouse get its energy?

From the monarch butterfly, which got its energy from a flower, which got its energy from the sun.

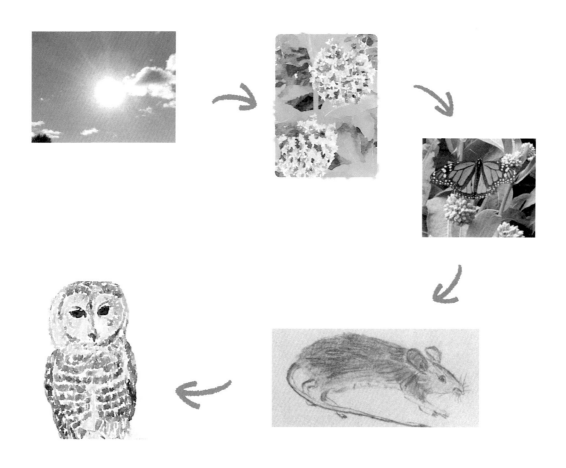

But that's not all.

One day the owl died from old age. Its body decomposed on the forest floor. First fungi and bacteria broke it down, then decomposers like worms, sow bugs, beetles, millipedes and slugs further broke it down. The insects and bacteria got their energy from the owl. And where did the owl get its energy?

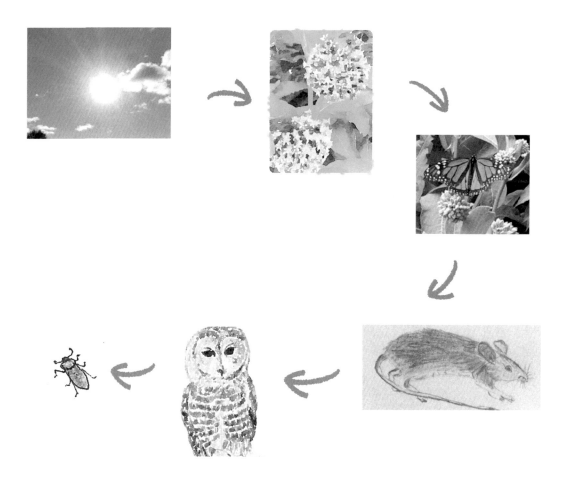

From the mouse, which got energy from the monarch butterfly, which got its energy from a flower, which got its energy from the sun.

But that's *still* not all.

The sun warmed that patch of soil where the owl's body had decomposed. Nutrients from the owl's body returned to the soil to help another seed grow, perhaps another milkweed. That's an owl life cycle.

The owl was connected to the mouse, which was connected to the monarch butterfly, which was connected to the milkweed. They were all linked together. This is a food chain.

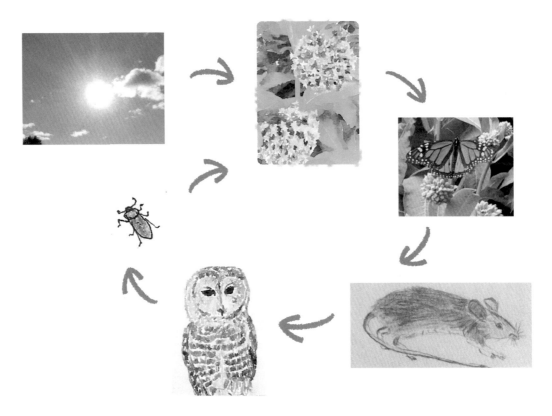

All food chains are possible because of energy from the sun.

Now do you think we're done?

Hint: Go back to the beginning.

Want to Know More?

All life needs energy to live. We need energy to grow, to play, to learn in school and to think. Plants and animals also need energy to grow and reproduce. Basically all life needs energy to complete their life cycles. We get our energy from the food we eat. Organisms that make their own energy with the help of the sun, such as plants, are called producers. Animals cannot make their own food energy from the sun in this way. This is different from making a sandwich. Yes, you put it together, but it's made from plants and maybe animals. Animals, including humans, are called consumers because they eat, or consume, other organisms. Consumers that eat only plants are called herbivores, while consumers that only eat other animals are called carnivores. When consumers eat both plants and animals, we call them omnivores.

Monarch butterfly populations have been declining. While there are several reasons for this, one of the biggest reasons is loss of habitat. Monarchs need milkweed plants for their larval stage. The milkweed plant is an obligate host, meaning it is the only food the monarch caterpillar can eat to survive.

Adult butterflies, however, can get nectar from many different flowers. The monarchs that migrate to Mexico each fall need nectar sources along their journey. Many of the places where wildflowers used to grow have been built up, so there is often not enough food energy to make the trip, or to have enough stored energy to survive the winter.

Monarchs that overwinter in Mexico need habitat too. Many of their forests are being cut down to grow crops.

What can you do? Plant some milkweed in your yard. Once it is established, it will come back every spring because it is a perennial plant. With more milkweed plants, hopefully the monarch butterfly will continue to return each spring.

And if you have space, allow fall wildflowers to bloom and provide food for those mighty travelers.

Still Curious? Check out Journey North:

https://www.learner.org/jnorth/tm/monarch/jr/ KidsJourneyNorth.html

Glossary

Chrysalis: a hard case that holds the pupa stage of a butterfly while it changes (metamorphoses) from the larva into an adult caterpillar.

Consumer: an organism that eats other living organisms to survive

Decompose: to break down into simpler forms of matter after death

Decomposer: an organism that breaks down the bodies of other organisms after they die

Food chain: the plants and animals linked together because of their relationships as producers and consumers

Larva: the worm-like stage of many insect life cycles; for moths and butterflies we call the larva a caterpillar

Metamorphose: to go through the process of changing form while growing; changing from a larva into an adult insect

Migrate: to move from one habitat or region to another as part of seasonal patterns or in search of food

Molt: to shed a layer of skin or feathers while growing

Nutrients: vitamins and minerals that organisms need for growth and health

Organism: a living being; an individual plant or animal

Producer: an organism, such as a plant, that makes its own food

Bibliography

Chapman, J. A. "Peromyscus Melanotis." *Mammalian Species* No. 764 (2005): 1-4.
   <http://www.science.smith.edu/msi/pdf/764_Peromyscus_melanotis.pdf>.

Eastman, John. *The Book of Field and Roadside: Open-country Weeds, Trees, and
   Wildflowers of Eastern North America.* Mechanicsburg, PA: Stackpole, 2003.

Fath, Brian D., and Geir Halnes. "Cyclic Energy Pathways in Ecological Food Webs."
   Ecological Modelling 208.1 (2007): 17-24.

"Monarch Butterflies." *Monarch Butterflies.* N.p., n.d. Web. 20 June 2014.
   <http://video.nationalgeographic.com/video/butterfly_monarch>.

"Monarch Butterfly Migration | Journey North Citizen Science Project Tracks
   Spring and Fall Monarch Butterfly Migration." *Monarch Butterfly Migration |
   Journey North Citizen Science Project Tracks Spring and Fall Monarch Butterfly
   Migration.* N.p., n.d. <http://www.learner.org/jnorth/monarch/>.

"Monarch Butterfly Migration." *Monarch Butterfly Migration.* N.p., n.d.
   <http://www.monarch-butterfly.com/monarch-migration.html>.

Ostfeld, Richard. May 2014. Personal communication.

Wagner, David L. *Caterpillars of Eastern North America.* Princeton: Princeton UP,
   2005.

Meet the Author, Lisa Connors

Lisa loves exploring nature and writing stories. Best of all, she likes writing stories with nature in them. Her ideas often come from walks on her property in Virginia or from traveling with her husband Chris, a geologist. *Milkweed Matters: A Close Look at the Life Cycles within a Food Chain* is her first self-published book. Any illustration not attributed to Betty Gatewood is either one of Lisa's watercolor paintings or one of her own photos manipulated with the Waterlogue App. She once saw a monarch butterfly laying eggs and collected that whole plant to study the monarch's life cycle. Her first traditionally published book, *Oliver's Otter Phase* will be published by Arbordale Publishing in the fall of 2017. For more information, please visit her website: https://lisaconnors.wordpress.com/

Meet the Illustrator, Betty Gatewood

Instead of presenting the perfect specimen, Betty paints it as it is — the torn
and tattered American chestnut leaves, the bug-eaten witch-hazel leaves, a
foggy mountain snow-scape, or the austere grace of a dried winter mint. Many of the
milkweed and monarch illustrations are made from her photos and observations in
Shenandoah National Park. Frequently on her rambles, she is accompanied by her
husband Mark, who often suggests particular subjects to document with her art. The
Shenandoah Valley, Appalachian Trail, Shenandoah National Park, and New England
are her favorite places to experience and document the beauties and intricacies of the
natural world. For more information, please visit her website:
http://www.gatewoodgraphics.com/
Betty used watercolors to paint these illustrations: